C000178353

The amazing story of . . .

Jesus in the Fathers

Patriarchs & Promises

Genesis 12–50

Published by PUSH Publishing 2017

www.pushpublishing.co.uk

in partnership with Jesus Centred Bible

office@jesuscentred.org

www.jesuscentred.org

Copyright © Christen Forster, 2017

All rights reserved. No part of this publication may be
reproduced, stored in a retrieval system, or transmitted
in any form or by means, electronic, mechanical,
photocopying or otherwise, without the prior written
consent of the publisher. Short extracts may be used for
review purposes.

Scripture quotations are based on the World English
Bible (WEB) which is in the public domain.
The WEB is a 1997 revision of the American Standard
Version of 1901.

A catalogue record for this book is
available from the British Library

ISBN-13: 978-0-9933445-7-2

Printed and bound in Great Britain by Cambrian Printers

Cover design by Joseph Laycock

Contents

Introduction   1

Using these notes   4

Part 1
The Spirit-Marked Family   7

Part 2
Abraham's Fatherhood, Failure and Faith   19

Part 3
Isaac's Witness as a Type of Christ   57

Part 4
Jacob's Journey   69

Summary   89

Dedication

I want to dedicate this book to Ann Handford, whose faithful service has kept this series happening through a tough season.

And thanks to the partners who gave me the time to write while I recovered last year: Dessie and Steve Poole, Tom and Lindsey Lillie, Jon and Heather Davis, Bob and Mary Bain, Tom and Annette Curtis, Florence Peters, Grahame and Gill Robinson, Jon and Alison Sworn, Dawn Tagg, Andy McNeil, Georgian and Winnie Banov.

A special thanks to my sister Debbie for checking my Hebrew and my brother-in-law Joe whose planning and artistic eye have got these books moving again. Finally my wife Judith, who is the real writer in the family!

Introduction

> Where is the **promise** of His coming? From the day that the **Fathers** fell asleep, all things continue as they were from the beginning of the creation . . . (But) the Lord is not slow concerning His **promise** . . . **2 Peter 3:4, 9b**

Peter wrote to those who looked for Jesus' return. They could look back on His birth, His ministry and the victory of His death, and find these events hidden from the opening chapters of the Bible – we explored this in Volume 2 *Jesus in the Beginning*. But now they looked forward to a promised second coming (*parousia*), could they find that too? Well yes actually!

We have already seen the parallels between the Creation story and the book of Revelation and, by the time Genesis has ended, two of the Patriarchs have modelled the life of Jesus in *two* distinct phases, implying a second coming or *parousia* ('presencing').

1

Paul once said, 'We preach to you the Good News of the promise made to the fathers', **Acts 13:32**. The *promise* of Jesus is *all* there in Genesis, albeit as 'seed'.

In this book we will explore the promise of Jesus in the lives of Abraham, Isaac and Jacob and his sons. Their stories are told in **Genesis 12 to 50**. This whole second half of Genesis is set up with the Genesis *Toledot* formula, where the word 'generations' breaks the book of Genesis into subsections. In Greek 'generations' is roughly translated 'Genesis', but the original Hebrew word is said *Toledot* (see *Jesus in the Beginning*).

But this generations section is not headed up by Abraham as we might think, rather Abraham's father is honoured as the source of his household, the Patriarchs:

> These are the generations of Terach . . .
> **Genesis 11:27**

We saw in *Jesus in the Beginning* that while the pagan name 'Terach' may have meant something like a 'wild goat' or 'a wanderer', to the Hebrew ear it sounded like the word for 'breath / spirit' with the marker letter *tav* at the beginning making the name imply 'very spirited' or 'marked by the spirit'.

In the beginning, the Spirit of God was brooding over the primal waters, **Genesis 1:2**, to nurture God's words of creation into being. Now at the start of the Patriarchs' stories we find a family 'marked by the Spirit' to bring about God's plan for salvation.

Salvation has always been *by faith* and faith always involves waiting with expectation for something we don't yet have, **Romans 8:24**. Faith is a response to whatever level of revelation of Jesus we do have, whether big or small, clear or ambiguous. Faith comes by hearing, and hearing by the Word of Christ, **Romans 10:17**.

When we come to the Fathers, we find that: Abraham saw Jesus' day and rejoiced *by faith,* **John 8:56**; Isaac, despite his preference for Esau, saw that the promised line was through Jacob *by faith,* **Hebrews 11:20**; and Jacob closes the book of Genesis by expressing the object of his *faith* in a word, *Yeshua* / ישוע which means 'Salvation' and is the Hebrew form of the name 'Jesus'.

> I have waited for your Jesus / ישוע, *YHWH*!
> **Genesis 49:18**

Jacob waited for Jesus just as we do . . . but the gift of hindsight allows us to see Jesus so much more clearly in their stories than the Fathers ever did. Perhaps in doing so we will be inspired to live lives that reflect Christ as we wait for Him too.

Using these notes

These mini-books are designed to shed light on your own personal study. You will get the most out of them if you mark up your own Bible as you see Jesus hidden in the texts we will cover. Over time as you read and re-read the Bible, the signposts you add today will help you find Jesus in new ways tomorrow, ideas will connect in your own understanding of the Life at the centre of everything.

The books will highlight the different ways Jesus is revealed in the Old Testament with reference to the seven streams I've settled on over the years. Note: the seventh icon works alongside the other six, it is not really a stream in its own right.

In my Bible each is colour-coded and has an easy to draw icon for when I don't have my coloured pencils. You will find the seven icons on the opposite page – you are welcome to use them if they are helpful.

Prophecy: Predictive, Ecstatic and Formative

 Typology: Models, Titles, People and Events

 Teaching: Used by Jesus/Gospels

 Jesus' Household: The Family Tree

 Trinity and Divinity: Jesus as God / God as a Plurality

 Christophanies: God in visible form

 Cryptic: Hidden in the Hebrew

Part 1

The Spirit-Marked Family

The Book of the Generations of Terah   9

Famous Names in the Line from Shem   10

The Joy of Isaac   12

The Book of the Generations of Terah

Terach is an epilogue to the Creation and Primeval History section of Genesis (see Volume 2, *Jesus in the Beginning*) and a prologue to the Patriarchs and Promises section, which we will cover in this volume.

All Terach's named children, Abram, Sarai, Nahor and Haran, are involved in Jesus' genealogy through Judah (as shown in the family tree below) – something you can't say of any other Patriarch. Like the Holy Spirit, who his name implies, Terach hovers invisibly but significantly behind the scenes of Jesus' history.

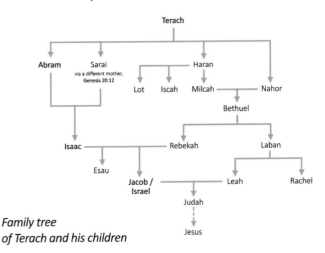

Family tree of Terach and his children

In Jewish tradition, Terach was a pagan idol maker who is saved by Abram's wisdom and faith, but the Bible affirms him as worshipping the same God as Abram, **Genesis 31:53**. He was descended from Noah's son Shem, who is acknowledged by Noah as following *YHWH*, **Genesis 9:26**.

⑫ Famous Names in the Line from Shem

Now 'Shem' means 'name', or figuratively 'fame' or 'renown'. While the people of Babel were busy chasing fame and a name by their own exploits, **Genesis 11:4**, God was already preparing a family that would become more famous than any family before or since.

Jacob is the twelfth Patriarch in the line of Shem, in fact Shem was still alive when Jacob was born. These twelve Patriarchs from Shem to Jacob find a mirror in Jacob's twelve sons, each of whom is a father to a tribe within the dynasty of Abraham. The number **twelve** is used in scripture to symbolise God's delegated authority or direction through human agents.

So in addition to the twelve Patriarchs in the line of Shem and the twelve sons of Jacob, there are also twelve Judges in the book of Judges. Jesus chooses twelve disciples, then the Holy Spirit births the church, clothing it with power only once there are twelve leaders in place,

Matthias taking the place of Judas, **Acts 1:23–26**.

Perhaps there is a connection between the symbolic meaning of the number twelve and the twelfth letter of the Hebrew alphabet, the letter Lamedh-ל. The pictogram that became the letter Lamedh-ל was based on the shepherd's crook, the means by which the shepherd saved, directed and corrected his flock. When used as a prefix, the letter Lamedh-ל adds the meaning of 'to' or 'towards' to a noun. There is clearly something of direction, leadership and shepherding associated with the Hebrew number / letter **twelve**.

Now back to Shem. We saw in the previous book in this series how the meaning of the names of Noah's ancestors from Shem to Abram made a sentence that anticipated a renowned healer or releaser:

> The renown / fame (**Shem**) *of the* healer-releaser (**Arphachsad**) sent (**Selah**) *from* the other side (**Eber**) *of the* divide (**Peleg**): a friend (**Reu**), a branch / vine (**Serug**), a lamp (**Nahor**) a wanderer/marked by the Spirit (**Terach**), raised by the Father (**Abram**).

That final phrase 'raised by the father', is a legitimate way of translating *Ab* / 'father' + *ram* / 'raised', though 'Abram' is normally translated as 'Exalted Father'. You get a feel for the clever way that ancient Hebrew works if you notice that symbolically the first letter in *'Ab'*, the Aleph-א, implied 'first' or 'source' and in Hebrew's original pictographic alphabet it was drawn as an ox-head 𐤀 which symbolized 'strength' or 'power'. The second letter Beth-ב meant 'household', and was originally drawn as an enclosed space or tent ◻. So 'Father' pictographically meant the the 'Strength of the tent / household'.

In the previous mini-book we stopped with Abraham. But we should allow Isaac and Jacob / Israel into the prophecy alongside Abraham, they too are Fathers to the whole nation of Israel. They bring the list of names through Shem to twelve. The twelve generations from Shem creates a balance with the twelve sons of Jacob who follow on.

The Joy of Isaac

Now Isaac is a straightforward name to translate – it means 'laughter' or 'laughing'. We see in this name another quality associated with Jesus. The New Testament makes Jesus' happiness a mark of his Messiah-ship. Applying **Psalm 45:7**, the writer of Hebrews, speaking of Jesus says:

> God, your God has anointed (messiah-ed) you with oil of joy / gladness more than your associates. **Hebrews 1:9**

The Hebrew word used for 'joy' in **Psalm 45** is very specifically linked with a prophetic image introduced by Jeremiah. That image was 'the Bridegroom', along with his 'Bride', whose voice or sound is described four times as 'the sound of joy'. The sound of joy is of course laughter, or Isaac.

> The sound of **joy**, and the sound of gladness, the sound of the **bridegroom**, and the sound of the bride.
>
> **Jeremiah 7:34, 16:9, 25:10 and 33:11**

Jesus took Jeremiah's symbolic figure, the Bridegroom, and applied it to Himself (**Matthew 9:15, Mark 2:20, Luke 5:35**) warning of a time when He would be 'taken away' and His disciples would mourn Him.

The first three times Jeremiah refers to 'the Bridegroom', it is the loss of the sound of laughing that is in view. But the final time it is a promise of its return, **Jeremiah 33:11–12**. Then, when the Bridegroom's happy sound is heard again, says Jeremiah, the world will recognise the 'Branch of David', the perpetual King and perpetual Priest and Jerusalem will finally have peace, **Jeremiah 33:14–18**.

In Jesus' day, no connection had been made between Jeremiah's Bridegroom and the Messiah, perhaps because the Bridegroom was more linked to being cut off than to the celebrations of God's fulfilled promises. John the

Baptist first applies the title to Jesus, **John 3:29**, and Jesus takes it up, but like Jeremiah, He warns of coming sadness when He is taken away:

> But days are coming when the Bridegroom will be taken from them, and then they will fast.
>
> **Mark 2:20** (see also **Matthew 9:15, Luke 5:35**)

As the New Testament progresses the focus shifts, as it does in Jeremiah, to the return of the Bridegroom's joy. The book of Revelation finally detailing the promised marriage of the slain Lamb, His rescued Bride and the peace of the New Jerusalem. Laughter is the sound of resurrection and the second coming:

> Looking to Jesus . . . who for the joy set before Him endured the cross . . . **Hebrew 12:2**

The Bridegroom's laughter becomes a symbol of Jesus' second coming. Here in Genesis we find it in seed form in the name Isaac and in the testimony it is a part of the family line from Shem.

So adding Isaac's name after Abram's gives us the phrase:

> *Raised by the Father (**Abram**) Laughing (**Isaac**) . . .*

Finally we need to add Jacob to this prophetic list of ancestral names, to fully see what the healer sent from the other side of the divide will really be famous for.

Jacob / יעקב comes from the word for 'heel' / עקב. The noun is used broadly for anything that is the last or lowest part of something, figuratively it can be something that 'follows on' or 'supplants' and it can mean 'crafty' or 'deceptive' as in tripping someone up. Jacob models all of these.

But *YHWH* gives Jacob a new name, Israel. And it is this name that so aptly fits the prophetic flow of ancestor names. 'Israel' has two parts, the second 'El' being simply 'God', but the first part 'Isra' has a variety of connected words and meanings that fall into three possible groups denoting: ruling, surviving or struggling.

Traditional sources give meanings for the name Israel such as:

- 'Prince of God' or 'God's Governor'
  (*Jones' Dictionary of Old Testament Names*)

- 'God persists' or even 'God survives'
  (*BDB Theological Dictionary*)

- 'Strives with God', 'God contends' or 'God's struggle'
  (*NOBSE Study Bible Names List*).

All three translation possibilities fit the history and destiny of Jacob and work in different ways in the prophetic flow of names:

> *Raised by the Father laughing, God's ruler / God Survives / God's Struggle . . .*

The first option is the simplest statement of fact, Jesus is 'God's Ruler'. The second is the most profound, 'God Survives', ie the Cross. And the third, 'God's struggle' tells us the meaning of the Cross.

If we take an aspect of each possibility, we would have:

> *Raised by the Father (**Abram**) laughing (**Isaac**), God's ruler contends and survives (**Israel**) . . .*

But perhaps, for simplicity's sake, we should opt for the plain reading, so the very spirited family line from Shem to Jacob tells us:

> *The renown of the healer sent from the other side of the divide: A friend, a vine, a lamp, very spirited, raised by the Father laughing as God's ruler.*

We will meet three more generations of Jesus' ancestors before the end of Genesis, but Jacob is the last full Patriarch and Genesis ends with his death and funeral, so we will wait before we think about what the names 'Judah', 'Perez' and 'Hezron' add to our unfolding prophecy of the promised Son. Already we are seeing the first hints of the ascended Jesus, but for now let's look at Abram's story.

This is a good point to transfer some notes into your Bible

Part 2

Abraham: Source of the Household of Faith

The Not-So-Great Father   21
Seven Visitations   23
Abraham's Philosophical Legacy   52
Abraham's Coda   53

The Not-So-Great Father

There is a tragic irony in Abram's name meaning 'great father' as in the natural he was a terrible father and a bad husband too, but as a man of faith he was certainly 'raised up by the Father' (my preferred translation of his name) to found a family that would change the world.

As a husband, Abram twice uses Sarai his wife (and half-sister) as a bargaining chip, a woman to be traded in marriage for his own safety and security of passage. In desperation, a childless Sarai lets Abram raise a surrogate child through her maid, but it seems Abram let his connection with Hagar become more than purely physical. Sarai challenges him, *'Let the Lord judge between you and me'*, **Genesis 16:5**, and Abram abdicates his responsibility to put things right by telling Sarai, *'she's in your hands . . . do what's good in your view'*, **Genesis 16:6**. Sarai kicks pregnant Hagar out and Abram does nothing for his unborn son. Hagar returns and gives birth to Ishmael, but years later after Sarai's own son Isaac is born, Sarai again kicks Hagar and Ishmael out. Abram is not being a great father.

It is during this period that *YHWH* changes Abram's name to 'Abraham' or 'Father of Nations', a more apt name perhaps than 'Great Father'. (Note: 'Abraham' doesn't actually mean 'Father of Nations' in a plain sense, but it has come to us as meaning this because of the fulfilment of the promises God makes to Abraham.)

As Abraham's story draws to a close he acquires his first piece of the land that *YHWH* has promised to him in full. It is a small plot for Abraham and his family to be buried in. From a natural perspective, Abraham's life is pretty average, but from a spiritual one he is the 'Father of Faith' for most of the world, whether Jewish, Muslim or Christian. That is because Abraham's life is shaped by seven visitations or revelations with promises from *YHWH* (see table opposite).

Now we saw in Volume 2 *Jesus in the Beginning*, the number seven did not so much imply the completion of something as it was the full promise of something yet to be fulfilled. Abraham's seven revelations / visitations imply a final revelation / visitation within his line and legacy. In fact, we can see Jesus in the shadows and shapes of Abraham's story throughout. For instance that field he bought in Canaan meant that 'by faith', Abraham's family could be buried in *YHWH*'s promise, just as 'by faith' we are buried with Christ, **Colossians 2:12**.

So let's take a closer look at Abraham's key moments from a deliberately Christocentric / Christotelic point of view and see what they show us.

7 visitations / revelations with promises from YHWH to Abraham

Location	Message via	Things promised / added	Genesis
Mesopotamia, before Haran, See **Acts 7:2**	*YHWH* speaks	To found a great nation, to have a great name, to be blessed and to bless.	12:1–3
Oak of Moreh	*YHWH* appears	A unique descendant, who will receive the world.	12:7
Canaan	*YHWH* speaks	This descendant's land will be eternal, Abram's descendants generally will be as numerous as dust.	13:14–17
Oaks of Mamre	Word of *YHWH* appears	A physical heir, not just a legal heir, heavenly descendants like the stars. The Promised Land is defined.	15:1–21
Unspecified	*YHWH* appears	Circumcision given as a sign, the cutting off of the flesh, Sarah will be a mother.	17:1–22
Oaks of Mamre	*YHWH* appears as three people	Abraham's future family are to model 'righteousness and justice'.	18:1–33
Mountain of Moriah	The Angel of YHWH	God swears by Himself to accomplish everything He has promised Abraham.	22:15–18

ⓐ *Visitation 1*

A Nation and a Name, to be Blessed and to Bless – Genesis 12:1–3

At the beginning of **Genesis 12**, *YHWH* speaks to Abram. The encounter is described after Terach has left Ur then settled and died in Haran, **Genesis 11:31–32**. But **Acts 7:2** tells us the revelation happened before Abram set out from Ur. Perhaps it was the reason the whole family set out for Canaan in the first place.

YHWH tells Abram to 'go' and that if Abram does go, a seven-fold promise will come into play. The first three folds of this promise are for Abram, the last three for everyone else and the middle fold explains how blessing will flow through Abram.

> I will make you a great nation
>> I will bless you
>>> I will make your name great
>>>> ***You shall be a blessing***
>>> I will bless those that bless you
>> The one who curses you will be bound under a curse
> In you all the families of the earth shall be blessed.

In this first visitation, there is no explicit mention of an heir, either earthly or heavenly, just a flow of blessing to

Abram, but ultimately through him for everybody. But there is something to notice.

Genesis 12:1–3 is the first recorded message spoken directly by *YHWH* to an individual since He spoke to Noah and his family declaring a 'new covenant' after the flood, **Genesis 9**.

Those words were spoken on the mountains of Ararat, which we saw in the last book can mean: *'a curse reversed'* or *'a curse turned over'*. These promises spoken 400 years later to Abram are *YHWH*'s first words on the details of how He is reversing the curse. They introduce a blessing that runs counter to the curse and consequence of the fall and hint at a mechanism for the whole world to access that blessing.

There is a pattern of pairs in this seven-fold promise, which I have highlighted using superscripts as follows:

When mankind left Eden[a] they left in an eastward[b] direction, **Genesis 3:24, 4:16**, into a world under a curse[c] in which the raising of children would be difficult. Now *YHWH* calls Abram back westward[b'], to be given a new land[a'], to experience blessing[c'] and to release blessing[c'] to the whole world, there is even an implied large family[d'] in the promise of becoming a nation.

The curse is being turned over!

This is a good point to transfer some notes into your Bible

 Visitation 2

The Great Tree that points the way — Genesis 12:6–7

Abram obeys *YHWH* and takes Sarai his wife and Lot his nephew and sets out not knowing where he will end up. But as they pass through Canaan, they come to Shechem where *YHWH* appears visibly to Abram. This visitation is described in a single verse, but it is one that is full of significance.

Genesis 12:7 is the first time that God has *appeared* to someone since He walked with Adam in the Garden in Eden. An appearance of God is always a 'Christophany', a pre-incarnation appearance of 'Christ', because it has always been the Son that has revealed the invisible God, **John 1:18.**

Now, the specific place where God the Son meets Abram is called the 'Oak of Moreh' ('Plain of Moreh' in KJV). *YHWH* clarifies His previous promise by confirming that *this* is the land that He is giving to Abram.

Now almost all Hebrew Lexicons will translate the place name 'Moreh' as 'teacher'. It is from a root-word meaning to point things out, (the root is also used for things that point such as 'rain' or 'archers'). This tree pointed out the promised land. It was a sign-post into it.

'Oak tree' or 'great tree' is the usual translation of the word אלון / Elwn. You will notice Elwn has the word 'el' in it, which (as well as meaning 'God') implies strength or pre-eminence, which is why it is an oak tree or a great tree.

The last time *YHWH* had appeared to anyone, He was walking among the trees in the garden He had given to Adam. This time He appears at the 'great tree of the teacher' or 'the god-tree that points the way' into the land He is going to give to Abram.

The 'Oak of Moreh' foreshadows the Cross, the great tree of the teacher Jesus that marks the way into all the promises of God!

At the 'Oak of Moreh', *YHWH* specifically adds a single phrase to His previous promise to Abram: 'to your *seed* I will give this land'. The promise of children is now explicit. **Genesis 12:7** is the first reference in the Bible to 'Abraham's seed'.

Now many modern translations of the Bible use the word 'descendants' in this verse rather than 'seed' emphasising the collective nature of 'Abraham's seed' in this and subsequent verses. But in doing so they are contradicting Paul who writes:

> Now the promises were spoken to Abraham and to his 'seed'. He doesn't say, to 'seeds,' as of many, but as of one, to your 'seed,' which is Christ. **Galatians 3:16**

The Hebrew word translated as 'seed'/'descendants' is a singular noun, zera/זרע, however like the English word 'sheep', it can be used as a true singular noun or as a collective singular noun, in other words it could be 'seed' or 'seeds'. So why is Paul so sure that 'Abraham's seed' should be understood as the singular descendant Jesus?

Paul can make his claim with confidence because 'Abraham's seed' had been understood as singular for hundreds of years. The Hebrew text of **Genesis 22:17** (for instance) refers to this 'seed' using the singular pronominal suffix with the subsequent noun, in this case the word is 'enemies' – they are 'his enemies' not 'their enemies'. Many English translations don't reflect the implication of a singular 'seed' in this and other Abrahamic passages that clearly have a specific heir in view, even if all heirs can claim some of the blessings.

We find the same tension in the description the 'Woman's seed', **Genesis 3:15**. The seed here is a 'He' not a 'They'.

All of God's promises to Abram will find their ultimate fulfilment in a single descendant who by implication is the same descendant promised to Eve who would crush the serpent's head.

There are just two more things to note about **Genesis 12:7**. First, there is the little marker word את in the middle of this promise – the aleph-א and tav-ת were the first and last letters of the Hebrew alphabet, and were the Jewish equivalent to alpha and omega in Greek. Second, the Hebrew word for 'land', *erets* / ארץ, is also the word for the whole world.

ה:זאת	ה:אץ	את	אתן	ד:ערז:ל
This one	The World / Land	Aleph– Tav	I shall give	To descendant of you

To your descendant Aleph-Tav (the first and last) I shall give this World

Abram would one day have an heir who was and is, 'the first and the last' inheritor of the whole world, and as the Bible concludes:

> . . . My reward is with me . . . I am the Alpha and the Omega, the first and the last, the beginning and the end. **Revelation 22:12–13**

This is a good point to transfer some notes into your Bible

 Visitation 3

An eternal heir – Genesis 13:14–17

The third time *YHWH* speaks to Abram is to reassure him in his failure. Straight after his previous visitation and promise Abram had left the land God was giving him and tried to pass off his wife as his sister.

God re-affirms that all the land Abram can see *will* belong to his seed (singular), and adds a new detail to the prophecy. This individual will own the land / world 'forever', **Genesis 13:15** – there is something eternal about Abram's promised descendant.

YHWH also draws Abram's attention to his wider descendants, these will be like the 'dry earth' or 'dust' which can't be numbered, **Genesis 13:16**. *YHWH* will make Abram the natural father of a people too numerous to number and of one particular heir who will own the world forever.

The Order of Melchizedek – Genesis 14

Abram moves to Hebron and builds an altar, which he shared with the family of an Amorite man called Mamre. English translations call this family 'allies', but the Hebrew is more specific, they 'own a covenant' with Abram.

While in Hebron, a raiding party of four northern kings routs five southern kingdoms including Sodom where Abram's nephew Lot now lives. Lot is captured. Abram and his allies, Mamre and his brothers, pursue the raiders, defeat them and rescue all those captured as slaves, including Lot.

On Abram's return, he is met by two kings. The first is Bera, King of Sodom. Abram has rescued the people and goods that Bera was unable to protect, Bera owes Abram. The second is Melchizedek the Priest-King of Salem. Melchizedek owes Abram nothing, his town and people were untouched by the raiders.

Melchizedek means 'King of Righteousness', as King of *Salem* he is also King of 'Peace'. He is described as Priest of *El Elyon* or 'God most High' and as a Priest he shares bread and wine with Abram. In return, Abram acknowledges Melchizedek as his priest by giving a tithe of his wealth to him. Abram also refuses payment for his actions from Bera King of Sodom, but does give a reward to his allies.

Abram is beginning to step into his prophesied role as the releaser of blessings and rebukes for nations and families, **Genesis 12:3**.

But the real significance of this incident is the intrusion of Melchizedek, a priestly King of Peace and Righteousness. He appears from nowhere with no ritual or family history, to offer 'communion' to Abram as he takes his first natural steps into the calling God had first spoken over him in Ur.

The book of Hebrews in the New Testament makes an explicit prophetic connection between Melchizedek and Jesus, quoting from **Psalm 110** which had already made a connection between Melchizedek and the coming Messiah. David starts this Psalm with the words:

> The LORD (*YHWH*) said to my Lord (*Adonai*), 'Sit at my right hand' . . . **Psalm 110:1**

David goes on to say:

> The LORD (*YHWH*) has sworn . . . you are a Priest forever of the order of Melchizedek.
> **Psalm 110:4**

Jesus Himself points out the paradox here – The Messiah will be David's son and yet David sees him as pre-existent sitting at *YHWH*'s right hand! **Matthew 22:43-45.**

At His trial, Jesus blends the imagery of **Psalm 110:1**, the Lord sitting at *YHWH*'s right hand with **Psalm 80:17** where the 'Son of Man' is the 'man of God's right hand'.

> You shall see the Son of Man *sitting at the right hand of Power* and coming on the clouds of Heaven. **Matthew 26:64**

It is this statement, drawing truth from **Psalm 110**, that condemns Jesus to death. There is not the space in this mini-book to follow all of the prophetic threads in this statement of Jesus, but if you have time you might like to investigate the imagery of the 'Mercy Seat' surrounded by clouds (which also gets picked up in the New Testament with reference to Jesus). Here we will simply notice that in **Psalm 110**, this pre-existing King is also an eternal Priest, '*of the order of Melchizedek*'.

Since the days of the Early Church, thinkers have debated and argued over whether Melchizedek is a prophetic *type* of Christ, or something more, perhaps the pre-existing Priest-King Jesus is actually appearing in Abram's story. The Babylonian Talmud claims that Melchizedek was a title for Noah's son Shem, (Shem would have been about 470 years old at this point in Abram's life, but he lived to 600 according to **Genesis 11:10–11**). Both the Roman Catholic and Orthodox Churches have made Melchizedek a Saint.

Whoever he was and whether as a type of Christ or as a Christophany, Melchizedek makes a significant impact on scripture's prophetic vision of the Messiah who would act as both a King and as a Priest. And that is despite only appearing twice by name in the whole Bible! Now there is a bit more related to the phrase '*of the order of* Melchizedek' as we shall see in the following section.

This is a good point to transfer some notes into your Bible

 *Visitation 4*

The Word of Living Promise — Genesis 15

The fourth time God makes a promise to Abram, He comes as '*The Word of YHWH*'. This is the first explicit visitation of this most important manifestation of God *The Word* into His creation. It is also the only time 'the Word' appears in Genesis.

In Volume 2 *Jesus in the Beginning,* we explored the development in Jewish thought of the idea that God's message into creation was an independent active agent, an agent the Targums called the *Memra*. We saw how

God's *words* caused creation and how His voice walked in the Garden. But by far the most important way of referring to this active agent in the Old Testament is as the *Dabar YHWH / דנר יהוה* – 'The Word of *YHWH*'.

As a title, *Dabar YHWH* is used over 250 times. This 'Word' is often visible, **1 Samuel 3:21**, **Micah 1:1**, and touchable, **1 Kings 18:31** (as a commentary on **Genesis 32:24–30**). The 'Word' even becomes incarnate in people's stories.

Note, **Jonah 1:1**, usually translated as:

> The Word of *YHWH came to* Jonah the son of Amittai saying . . .

can also be translated as

> The Word of *YHWH BECAME* Jonah . . .

The little verb היה / *heyah* translated here as 'came' actually means to exist, to be or to become (see *Strongs* H1961). With Jonah, as with other prophets that the Word 'became', it is impossible to untangle the message from the messenger, they model the mystery of 'Christ in you'. See also **Hosea 1:1**, **Joel 1:1**, **Zephaniah 1:1** etc.

As a word, *dabar* the 'word' means more than just simple speech, Hebrew has a separate word-root for simple words and talk: *omer* / 'word' and *amar* / 'speech'. *Dabar* on the other hand is a considered word, the output of a thought process. Each of the Ten Commandments is called a *dabar*.

The Hebrew root *DBR* / דנר is found in other words in which consequence or depth is implicit too.

So, the reason or cause of something or the class that something belongs to is called the *DBRH* / דנרה, as in the '*order* of Melchizedek', **Psalm 110:4**, this eternal priestly order embodies the Word (see above).

And the Inner Sanctuary of the Temple, the Holy of Holies is called in Hebrew the *DBYR* / דניר, **1 Kings 6:19–23**. Because *DBYR* is an extension of *DBR,* ie 'the Word', the King James Bible calls this place 'the Oracle' despite it being described as a room in the temple. So the Holy of Holies, the *DBYR,* is perhaps best understood as the 'place of the Word' – the message it contains is the Mercy Seat on top of the Ark guarded by two angels. In the New Testament, Jesus (the Word made flesh) is called the Mercy Seat, **1 John 2:2,** because the Greek word here for 'propitiation'/ ἱλαστήριον is also used for the Mercy Seat in both the Septuagint and in **Hebrews 9:5**.

Genesis 15 is the first place we meet the 'Word' who will one day become flesh in a way that lives among us, that models an eternal Priesthood and who comes in the clouds seated on the Mercy Seat in the Holy of Holies (to blend the imagery of **Psalms 80** and **110**). Here in **Genesis 15**, the Word is already solid enough that he can lead Abram outside and show him the stars (v5), then have animals brought to him (v9–10).

Abram's Faith in Jesus

It is here in the middle of the fourth and central promise of seven to Abram, as he interacts with the embodied Word, that Abram has his key moment of faith.

At the start of the chapter the Word has spoken a phrase we find so often in the mouth of Jesus in the Gospels: 'Fear not', see **Luke 8:50**.

The Word keeps speaking, promising to be a shield and a reward to Abram and explaining that Abram would have a natural born heir, not just an adopted heir. Then the Word leads Abram outside and shows him the stars and promises him a huge number of heavenly descendants on top of the earthly descendants already promised.

Faith comes by hearing and hearing by the Word of Christ, so we read:

> Then He (the Word) said to him (Abram) . . . Then he (Abram) believed in *YHWH* and He (*YHWH*) counted it to him (Abram) as righteousness. **Genesis 15:5–6**

This verse is quoted four times in the New Testament as an example of saving faith, **Romans 4:3, 20–22, Galatians 3:6** and **James 2:23**. Abram's saving faith is in Jesus even though Abram doesn't know Him by that name. But Abram does acknowledge this key moment by introducing a new Trinitarian title for *YHWH*.

Multi-Lords-God

Abram responds to the active *Dabar YHWH*, by calling Him *'Adonai'*, **Genesis 15:2, 8**. This is the first use of this name for God in the Bible.

Adonai is often translated in English Bibles as 'Lord', with just the first letter capitalised to distinguish it from 'Lord', which is used for *YHWH*. *Adonai* is used just over 400 times in the Old Testament as a name or title for God. As a title, *Adonai* is informal but respectful, it is the equivalent calling someone 'sir' or adding the title 'mister' to their name. It comes from a root, *Adon* / אדן that means a base or pedestal and is used to imply authority.

Adonai / אדני adds the suffix yod– י to the root, giving translators a couple of options: *Adonai* could be first-person-possessive, 'my Lord'; or it could be masculine-plural, pertaining to someone or something, as in 'lords of mine'. In simple terms, that means that *Adonai* is how you would write 'lords of', 'my lord', 'my lords' and 'my lords of'. Translators use context to decide.

By calling *Dabar YHWH 'Adonai',* Abram hints at God's multi-
unity even before it's revealed as a trinity just two chapters
later in the form of three men. The Bible calls all three men
YHWH, **Genesis 18:13**, while Abram applies his plural name
Adonai to all three of them, see **Genesis 18:3.**

I like 'my Lords' as a translation that can be used in most
contexts. Here in Genesis 15 it would be, 'my Lords (of)
YHWH', and if we expanded *YHWH* it could be 'my Lords
of Living Promise' (see Volume 2, *Jesus in the Beginning*).

The one-sided covenant

God is halfway through making His sevenfold promise to
Abram, when Abram asks:

> Oh *Multi-Lord* of Living Promise, how can I know
> that I shall obtain this? **Genesis 15:8**

Despite the wavering implicit in the question, *YHWH*
honours Abram's previously expressed faith by giving
Abram an answer that serves as one of the most profound
types of the Cross in the Old Testament. God 'cuts' a
covenant with Abram and yet in the cutting process
God takes the curse implicit in the failure of *either* party
entirely on Himself. It was like *YHWH* adding the words '*I*
cross my heart and hope to die if *either of us* fails to see
this promise through to completion'.

The difference between a promise and a covenant is two-fold. First, there is an acceptance of the promise by the receiver complete with any restrictions or obligations implicit in the acceptance. Abram has accepted *YHWH*'s promise by faith just a few verses before.

Second, and consequentially, there is a necessary penalty for both parties if the promise fails.

In the ancient world, to add gravity to a received promise, an animal would be killed then both parties to the agreement would walk through the blood and pieces of its death. In doing so they were taking on a curse, represented by death, if either party failed to keep their side of the bargain.

So in response to Abram's question about how he can obtain the things God has already promised him, God tells Abram to kill not just one animal, but every type of sacrificial animal – cattle, flock animals and birds, to make an ultimate sacrifice.

But before Abram can walk through the pieces with God, a stupor falls on him and God tells him that the first evidences of this covenant will not be properly seen for another 400 years. Then God passes through this ultimate sacrifice on His own but as two distinct manifestations. As a smoking furnace, and as a firebrand.

400 years later Abram's earthly descendants would step into the first visible evidence of this covenant when they would be led through the Red Sea by the pillars of smoke and of fire, **Exodus 14:19–21**. Both are described in **Exodus 14** as manifestations of 'The Angel of *YHWH*' (a Christophany we are going to meet properly in the next chapter of Genesis) and Moses even calls this Angel 'Jesus':

> Fear not, stand back and see Jesus-of-Living-Promise / (salvation of *YHWH*) that He will show you today. **Exodus 14:13**

The word 'salvation' here is the name Jesus / ישוע marked with the little word את, a title of Jesus and implies a divine sacrifice on a cross as well as being the first and last letters of the Hebrew alphabet (see *Jesus in the Beginning*). If the columns of smoke and of fire are manifestations of Jesus in **Exodus**, then they are here too in **Genesis 15**.

Jesus, as fire and smoke, passes through death all by Himself but on behalf of a man and his future family. This is a covenant cut not on the basis of the faithfulness of both parties, but on the long-term faithfulness of one party in response to the momentary faith of the other. There is nothing that Abram need do to achieve the benefits of this promise, *YHWH* will even own the consequences of Abram's failures.

The Messenger of God — Genesis 16

Abram's significance in world history can't be overstated, he is the Father of Jews, Palestinians and Arabs alike. When *YHWH* appeared visibly to him as the 'Word' it seemed to confirm Abram's status. But in the next chapter *YHWH* appears again, as 'The Angel / Messenger of the Lord', this time it is to a seeming side character in the story, Hagar, Sarai's poorly treated and bonded maid-servant.

Hagar is quite certain she has seen *YHWH*, she names the Angel / Messenger, *Elroi*, which means 'God who sees' and exclaims:

> I have now seen Him who sees me.
> **Genesis 16:13b**

In my Bible I have highlighted this passage to remind me that Jesus is meeting with a poor, frightened, pregnant and abandoned girl face to face. The 'God who sees', has answered her frightened prayers.

This is another first appearance of an important Christophany. 'The Angel of *YHWH*' is not simply an Angel *from YHWH*. The Hebrew word מלך / *malak* means a 'messenger', the name Malachi is the same word.

Throughout the Old Testament this 'messenger' of *YHWH* carries *YHWH*'s presence and receives worship as if He is God and not simply a third party carrying a message.

The unknowable God is being made known through His knowable Son who is '*YHWH* the Word' and '*YHWH* the Angel'. Jesus is both the message (Word) and the messenger (Angel).

 This is a good point to transfer some notes into your Bible

Visitation 5

Abraham, Sarah and Circumcision – Genesis 17

The fifth time *YHWH* speaks to Abram, He changes Abram's name and the name of his wife Sarai to, Abraham and Sarah. Sarah is explicitly made a part of *YHWH*'s plan for Abraham's descendants, **Genesis 17:15–22**. Specifically, God's plans to bring in an everlasting covenant will happen through Sarah's son, who will be called Isaac.

Importantly *YHWH* gives Abraham a sign, an action of faith to be undertaken by the generations to come after him. That sign was circumcision, a deliberate cutting off or wounding of the flesh.

> And you shall be circumcised in the flesh of your

> foreskin and it shall be a sign of the covenant
> between me and you. **Genesis 17:11**

Now the word 'flesh' here is marked out with the definite direct object marker, the little word we encountered in the previous books in this series, *AT* / את, the first and last letters of the Hebrew alphabet. As we saw in *Jesus in the Old Testament*, the original proto-Sinaitic pictograms for the letters aleph-א and tav-ת were a bull-𐤀 and a cross-✝ respectively. The bull was both a symbol of the divine in the ancient world and the biggest acceptable sacrifice in Judaism, a bull could be offered up by fire over a criss-cross of sticks, but ultimately this little word breathes Jesus' ultimate, divine sacrifice on a cross throughout the whole Old Testament.

Also the word for 'sign', אות is this same little word *AT* / את with an extra letter in it, a wav-ו. 'Wav' means 'hook' / 'spike' / 'peg', and in ancient and modern Hebrew the letter looks like a nail.

Genesis has coded in a hidden truth here, circumcision is really about the cutting-off of the flesh of the eternal (first and last) divine sacrifice on a cross:

> You shall be circumcised in the A*T* / את / *flesh* of
> your foreskin and it shall be a AW*T* / אות / *sign*
> of the Covenant between Me and you.
>
> **Genesis 17:11**

The New Testament presents the crucifixion as Jesus' fulfilment of this physical sign:

> In Him you were also circumcised with the circumcision made without hands, by putting off the body of the sins of the flesh, by the circumcision of Christ . . . when you were dead in your sins and the uncircumcision of your flesh He made you alive . . . having cancelled out the debt . . . having nailed it to the cross. **Colossians 2:11–14**

Circumcision was always an outward sign that required an inner response.

> So circumcise the foreskin of your heart, and be stiff-necked no longer. **Deuteronomy 10:16** (see also **30:6** and **Jeremiah 4:4**)

Just as the Cross is a physical event that draws an inner or spiritual response by faith from us.

Abraham's Family and God's Tri-unity

Shortly after Abraham and his household are circumcised, *YHWH* appears to him again. This is Abraham's sixth visitation, *YHWH* appears as three men!

YHWH reaffirms his promise of a son through Sarah, but on this occasion, He reveals a bit more about how Abraham's family and household will achieve *YHWH*'s blessing on all nations.

> For I have chosen him (Abraham) in order that he may instruct his children and his household after him to keep the way of *YHWH* by doing *righteousness and justice*: in order that *YHWH* may bring upon Abraham, the things He has spoken about to him. **Genesis 18:19**

YHWH's ultimate objective, blessing the world, will happen because Abraham will create a family-based community that will try to live for *YHWH* and embody *righteousness* (inward morality) and *justice* (outward morality).

 YHWH brings this revelation in the form of three men, **Genesis 18:2**. The three are addressed in various combinations, by both Abraham and Lot, as *Adonai*, the plural but singular divine title used by Abraham the first time *YHWH* appeared to him as the Word, **Genesis 15:2**.

Note how the three men talk and act as if they are one person. So 'they said' becomes 'he said' which then becomes '*YHWH* said', **Genesis 18:9–13**. And we read 'But the men reached out their hand (singular)' in **Genesis 19:10**.

It is interesting to note how, as *YHWH*'s message to

Abraham becomes more focused on the family-community that *YHWH* wants to create through him, that *YHWH* reveals the trinity in His own heart most clearly too.

As the Old Testament develops towards the New we will see the characteristics of Father, Son and Holy Spirit (see below) appear within God's multi-unity, but here for the first time we see that one-ness as Tri-unity.

 This is a good point to transfer some notes into your Bible

Visitation 7

Abraham's faith and the beloved, promised, 'only Son'

The last time *YHWH* speaks to Abraham is the crescendo of Abraham's story. Isaac the promised son of Abraham and Sarah has been born and before *YHWH* speaks his final prophetic promise to Abraham, He first asks him to offer up Isaac as a sacrifice. There are elements of this story I want to look at later from the perspective of Isaac – here we will focus on the elements that best fit the climax of Abraham's story.

YHWH refers to Isaac as Abraham's 'only Son' (Ishmael is now gone), and as a 'beloved son', **Genesis 22:2**. The allusions to Jesus are obvious, and hidden in the Hebrew we find that little marker word *AT* / את attached to the words 'Only', 'Son' and 'Isaac'. In fact *AT* / את appears 28 times in the 19 verses of the story of the offering of Issac. It also marks out the words for: the wood that will form the altar, the altar, the knife that will pierce the sacrifice, the fire that will consume the sacrifice, the location that Abraham sees for the sacrifice and (perhaps most importantly) the substitute ram that is sacrificed in Isaac's stead.

This little untranslated marker word appears roughly eight times per page from start to finish of the Old Testament, but here, in the story of the offering of Isaac, one of the Bible's clearest typological representations of the sacrifice of Jesus, it appears with more than three times the usual frequency. If the 'את' breathed the concept of sacrifice through the whole of the Old Testament, here it shouts it in triplicate, the divine-prime-sacrifice-on-a-cross, being modelled in the lives of Abraham and Isaac.

Now, Abraham is told to offer Isaac on a mountain God will show him in the land of Moriah, **Genesis 22:2**.

Moriah is used as a place name just once more in the whole Bible, but the location is incredibly important, the Mountain in Moriah that *YHWH* shows Abraham becomes

'Mount Moriah' and it is the place that *YHWH* appears to David, and where Solomon builds the temple, see **2 Chronicles 3:1**. Ultimately, Jesus is crucified, buried and rises again on the slopes of Mount Moriah.

If you look up the place name Moriah in some older reference books, they make no attempt to translate the name, and *Jones' Dictionary of Old Testament Proper Names* links the name rather dubiously to the verb ראה / *rah* which is a part of the name of God revealed during this episode, *YHWH YRAH* / יראה, which is often said as 'Jehovah Jireh' and meaning '*YHWH* will see (to) it'. So *Jones'* translates Moriah as 'Visible of God', but this is not considered a good translation. This is all a bit odd given that the Hebrew is very straightforward.

Moriah is spelt slightly differently the two times it is used. On both occasions the second part is the same, it is simply the shortened form of God's Covenant name, *YAH* / יה.

The first part of the name is spelt here in **Genesis 18** as *m-r* / מר and in **2 Chronicles** as *myr* / מור, both of which are spellings of the word we translate as 'myrrh' – they are part of a root-word group that denotes things that are 'bitter' or 'strong' (bitter flavours are strong flavours in Hebrew just as spicy flavours are hot flavours in English).

Now 'bitterness', 'strength' and 'myrrh' all fit the location Moriah very well as we see its place in God's story develop. It is here that God asks Abraham to do a '*bitter thing*', it is here that Priests, anointed with *myrrh* and oil, would minister in the Temple, and it is here where both the *bitterness* and *strength* of God would be revealed in the paradox of the Cross, where power would be made perfect in weakness, **2 Corinthians 12:9**.

Eventually Nicodemus will wrap the broken body of God's only Beloved Son in bands anointed with so much *myrrh* (more than three year's-worth of an average wage, **John 19:39-40**) that the *bitter* smell must have wafted across the entire region of *Moriah* for at least three days.

 There is something poetically prophetic and instructive in this location name – **the Mountains of** *YHWH***'s Bitterness / Strength / Myrrh**.

So, as he walks in his own bitterness, 'On the third day Abraham raised his eyes and saw the place from afar', **Genesis 22:4**. With hindsight we can see Abraham looking down the years as well as across the distance and finding his hope in the distant future on the hill ahead of him, so when asked by Isaac about the lamb needed for the sacrifice, Abraham prophesies:

> God will see to it for Himself, the Lamb for the offering . . . **Genesis 22:8**

 Jesus will testify about this moment:

> Abraham rejoiced to see My day, he saw it and
> was glad. **John 8:56**

In response to Abraham's faith *YHWH* swears *'by Himself'* for the first and last time in the patriarchal stories to fully carry out His promised blessings on Abraham's family, to multiply Abraham's descendants both naturally, and spiritually, as sand and as stars, and He promises that a singular descendant / seed will:

> possess the gates of his enemies.
> **Genesis 22:17**

The possession is singular – '*HIS* enemies' – even though some English translations make it the plural 'their enemies'.

Abraham's story is coming to an end, the offering of Isaac is its climax, and while Abraham's adventure has finished, there is still a bit more revelation in his legacy.

 This is a good point to transfer some notes into your Bible

Abraham's Philosophical Legacy

We noted in Volume 2, *Jesus in the Beginning* how Jewish thinking at the time of Jesus was comfortable exploring the dynamic shape of God revealed by his Spirit and by His Word in the Old Testament. We saw that Philo, a philosopher / theologian living contemporaneously with Jesus, but in Alexandria in Egypt, had popularised the use of the Greek word 'Logos' for God's wisdom, which he also referred to as God's firstborn son.

On one occasion, Philo gives a list of ways the firstborn has been revealed which looks very much like it has been drawn from **Genesis 15 – 18**, where God appears physically to humanity for the first time since Eden.

> . . . to be adorned according to his **firstborn word** – the **eldest of his angels, as the great archangel**[1] of many names, for he is called: **the authority and the name of God**[2] (ie *YHWH*) and **the Word**[3], and **man according to God's image**[4], and **he who sees**[5] Israel . . .
>
> (*On the confusion of tongues*, Philo of Alexandria, 20 BC – 50 AD)

So note:

– **Genesis 15**: God appears as **the Word**[3]

- **Genesis 16**: God appears as the **Angel of** *YHWH*[1] and as **God who Sees**[5]

- **Genesis 17**: God appears simply as *YHWH*, **His Name and Authority**[2]

- **Genesis 18**: God appears represented by **three men**[4]

It might be tempting to think that seeing Jesus in these theophanies in Abraham's story is simply a case of wishful hindsight, a bit too smug and smart after the event. But Philo's words (above) were written perhaps before Jesus had started His ministry and certainly well before the Church had formulated its creeds. It is perhaps truer to the facts to understand that Jesus came at just the right time, as the cross-cultural winds blew the dust off the old familiar stories and challenged the best Jewish thinkers of Jesus' day to contemplate the need for God-the-Son.

Abraham's Coda

Abraham's story is nearly done. Over the next three chapters, **Genesis 23–25**, Sarah will die and Abraham will buy his first piece of the Promised Land as a burial plot for his family. Then Abraham will send out his oldest servant to find a wife for Isaac. In commissioning his servant Abraham makes his last recorded speech before he dies, some forty years later having taken a final wife, Keturah, see **Genesis 25:1,7**.

Abraham's function has been fulfilled, but God continues to bless him, and he lives to see his grandchildren, Jacob and Esau. And even in these final passages covering Abraham's twilight years there is a run of symbolic events that reflect and reveal Jesus typologically.

So note how in these chapters:

1) We are buried in hope! **Genesis 23**

Following the offering of his only beloved son, Abraham prepares a place so that all his future children can be buried in the hope of His promises, **Genesis 23:19–20**. Just as we are buried in Christ, that we may live a new life! **Romans 6:4**.

2) The Spirit gathers a bride from the nations. **Genesis 24**

Abraham then sends out his senior servant to collect a bride for his 'resurrected' son. This servant is presumably 'Eliezer of Damascus' who is described in **Genesis 15:2** as 'heir of my [Abraham's] house' – this Hebrew phrase can also be translated as 'servant/steward of my house'. The phrase 'of Damascus' is thought by most scholars to be a reference to a blood tie (Hebrew *dam* = 'blood') rather than to the place in Syria which didn't exist at the time – the word literally means 'sack of blood'. So it seems Abrahams heir was a servant with some form of blood relationship with Abraham.

'Eliezer' means 'God's Helper', so typologically this servant and his quest represents the Holy Spirit gathering a bride from the nations for the only Beloved Son of the great Father. We see the Trinity in Abraham (Great Father), Eliezer (God's helper) and Isaac (the only Son).

Rebekah meets the servant who gives her gifts. She agrees to the marriage to the only beloved son *by faith*. This all happens as Rebekah is collecting water from a well. We see the Church in Rebekah the bride, getting to know the Son through the mediating Holy Spirit.

3) Jesus in name and number

Now, spread across these simple but beautiful types of God the Father, Son, Holy Spirit, and the Church, we find the name Jesus hidden in a most unusual way.

You may remember in *Jesus in the Beginning* how we saw the connection between the את of **Genesis 1:1** and Jesus the Alpha–Omega of **Revelation 22**. We also saw how the value of the name 'Jesus' in Greek added up to 888 as a contrast to 'Nero Caesar', which in Hebrew added up to 666. Now if you take the name 'Jesus' in its Hebrew form, ישוע, it adds up to 386 (ע=70, ו=6, ש=300, י=10).

Unusually we find the name ישוע in reverse order spread out every 386 letters across these typological events of **Genesis 23–24** (remember when these events were first recorded, words could be written in either direction).

Rabbis love finding names spread out in the Hebrew text of the Bible, and it is treated as more significant if the spacing is the same number as the summation of the value of the letters in the name, as it is here. For those that want to mark this in their Bibles, the table below identifies the verse and word each letter appears in.

Letter	Verse	Compound Word
י	Genesis 24:16	'to-the-spring'
שׁ	Genesis 24: 10	'his-master'
ו	Genesis 24:3	'I-dwell'
ע	Genesis 23:15	'between'

This may just be a coincidence, but I'm sure God has always known it was there and, given that it was spotted by a Rabbi, Yacov Rambsel, working without the aid of a computer, it feels to me that the Lord must have known He was leaving a fingerprint for someone to find, evidence that points to the Holy Spirit's involvement in preparing the text of the Bible. It can be a sign to those who are seeking Jesus, even if it doesn't convince those that would rather not find Him.

Abraham's witness to Jesus is coming to an end — Isaac's is just beginning.

Part 3

Isaac: Seed of the Household of Faith

The Only Son   59
The Generations of Isaac   64

The Only Son

Isaac is called an only son despite having a brother – while the title might not have been technically true, it emphasises that he was the son through whom the Seed, God's only Son, would come. Interestingly the Hebrew word for son 'ben' / בנ is made up of two letters that tell a story, just as the word *Ab* / 'father' meant 'Source of the House'. As a pictogram, the letter beth-ב represented a 'tent' or 'household', ⊓. Nun-נ means 'continue' and was drawn in proto-siniatic pictograms as a seed, ⤸. So Isaac was the 'Seed of the household'.

Isaac's story is short compared with that of Abraham before him and Jacob and his sons after him. We have already seen a little of how he models Jesus as a type in offering himself as a sacrifice, and we have even glimpsed something of the ascended Christ as Eliezer (God's Helper) gathers a gentile wife for him.

What you may not have noticed though is how Isaac disappears from the story while Eliezer is acting on his behalf.

Abraham and Isaac go up the mountain of God's-Bitterness (Moriah) together, Isaac allows himself to be offered though God provides a ram in his place. But then *only* Abraham returns down the mountain, **Genesis 22:19**!

We assume Isaac is still around, but he is invisible in the text, he doesn't reappear until he receives the bride who has accepted him by faith in the testimony of God's Helper. Isaac is modelling how Christ is with us, but invisibly until He comes again to receive his bride, gathered from every nation by the work of the Holy Spirit.

The typological connections between Isaac and Jesus are so multi-layered that even though we have covered a lot of them it is worth listing them out in the three tables below, reflecting Jesus' Incarnation, His Sacrifice, and His Ascension.

This is a good point to transfer some notes into your Bible

Isaac models Jesus ' Incarnation

Isaac	Connection	Jesus
Genesis 22:2, 12, 16	Both were only, beloved sons	Matthew 3:17 John 3:16
Genesis 17:16	Both had their birth foretold to their fathers	Matthew 1:20–21
Genesis 18:10–15	Both had their birth foretold to their mothers	Isaiah 7:14, Luke 1:26–31
Romans 4:19 Hebrew 11:11	Both were miracle conceptions	Matthew 1:18
Genesis 18:12	Both had their conception questioned by their mother	Luke 1:34
Genesis 17:19	Both were divinely named	Matthew 1:21
Genesis 21:2	Both were born at just the right moment/God appointed time	1 Corinthians 15:8

Isaac models Jesus' Sacrifice

Isaac	Connection	Jesus
Genesis 22:2–3	Both were offered in sacrifice by the will of their Father while in the prime of life	Matthew 26:42
Genesis 22:9	Both accepted their role willingly . . .	John 10:17–18
Genesis 22:2	. . . In the hills of Moriah	John 19:20
Genesis 22:6	Both carried the wood for their own sacrifice . . .	John 19:17
Genesis 22:9	. . . Both were secured on that wood	Luke 23:33
Genesis 22:13	The head of the sacrifice was entangled in thorns	Matthew 27:29
Genesis 22:4	The hope of resurrection came on the third day	Matthew 17:23

Isaac models Jesus' Ascension and Return

Isaac	Connection	Jesus
Genesis 22:19	Neither return visibly from the mountain	Acts 1:9–12
Genesis 22:19 — 24:62–64	Both are absent until they receive their bride	Acts 1:12 Revelation 19:7
Genesis 24:2–4	Abraham commissions his servant (the Holy Spirit) to collect a bride for his son (Eliezer = God's Helper)	Revelation 21:9–10
Genesis 24:13,15 & 62–64	The bride is met at a spring first by the servant, then by the bridegroom himself	Revelation 22:17
Genesis 24:53	The servant gives the bride gifts	Hebrews 2:4
Genesis 24:57–58	The bride agrees to the marriage 'by faith'	Acts 26:18

The Generations of Isaac

The eighth *Toledot*, or 'Generations' section, of Genesis starts at **Genesis 25:19**:

> These are the generations of Isaac . . .

The action is immediate! Within three verses Rebekah has been barren, Isaac has prayed for her, she's conceived and found out that it's twins, and what's more the twins are fighting in the womb. So much so that Rebekah looks to *YHWH* for a word and receives one. The children's struggle is a foretaste of the prophetic sign to be revealed in the history of their future families.

 Esau and Jacob, and the nations they become, Edom and Israel, stand as important 'types' in the lexicon of prophetic symbolism.

Edom / אדום, the nation from red-haired Esau means 'red' but it is from the same root word as Adam / אדם. Edom becomes a symbol of the flesh, of the old humanity in Adam. Esau / Edom has a carnal entitled expectation of grace and favour that belongs to its own whit, works and lineage.

Jacob / יעקנ can mean 'crafty' or 'supplanter' but for now I want to focus on its root meaning of 'heel' / עקנ – Jacob is the 'bruised heel' (see **Genesis 3:15**) who becomes Israel /

ישראל, 'God's ruler'. Jacob–Israel stands in prophecy, if not always in practice, for faith-lived, grace-given election.

The flesh, Edom, with its natural successes is in constant competition with faith and its spiritual fruit born of divine–human co-operation.

So Edom is Israel's first opponent as they escape from Egypt in Exodus, **Exodus 17:8** (Amalek is Esau's grandson, and the Amalekites were a tribe of Edom). And as the Old Testament draws to a close, Edom is still called 'the people with whom *YHWH* is permanently displeased', **Malachi 1:4**. In between, Edom is Israel's constant sibling rival: King Saul is undone by Edom, **1 Samuel 15**, and an Edomite kills him at his end, **2 Samuel 1:8-10**; whereas David subjects Edom, **2 Samuel 8:14**, and brings them peace and justice along with Israel, **1 Chronicles 18:13–14**.

As Jesus is born, Herod (an Edomite) tries to kill Him. Herod the Great was the last King of Judea, but his parents were proselyte converts from Edom. At Jesus trial Herod's son Antipas, the Edomite king of Galilee, fails to intervene on Jesus' behalf, just as Edom the nation had ignored Israel in times of trouble:

> On the day that you [Edom] stood aloof / to the side . . . foreigners entered his [Jacob's] gate and casts / cast lots for Jerusalem, you too [Edom] were like one of them! **Obadiah 1:11**

This prophetic rivalry of Jacob and Esau is picked up in the New Testament too. We find it in **Hebrews 12:15–17** where believers are warned against Esau's carnal assumptions of grace. And Paul uses it in the middle of his defence of Salvation by Faith in **Romans 9**:

> My kinsmen according to the flesh . . . not all children are Abraham's true descendants, but: 'Through Isaac you children will be named' . . . And not only this but . . . '**Jacob I loved, but Esau I hated**' . . . pursuing a law of righteousness [Paul's kinsmen by birth] did not arrive at it. Why? Because it was not pursued by faith, but as though it was by works.
>
> **Romans 9:3c,7,10a, 13b,31b-32a**.

Seeing Esau/Edom as symbolic of the first Adam and the flesh, and Jacob/Israel as symbolic of the second Adam (Jesus) and faith, changes the way we read so many Old Testament passages. For instance, the last line of the birth prophecy regarding Esau and Jacob reads: 'the older shall serve the younger', **Genesis 25:23d**.

This doesn't simply mean that Israel would be a bigger nation than Edom, but that one day all flesh / humanity would find their place in faithful service of God's ruler, Jesus, **Philippians 2:10**.

Isaac's last testimony as a type of Christ is in his two children who show us that there are two ways of relating to the grace we receive. The whole book of Galatians addresses this conflict.

> Are you so foolish? Having begun with the Spirit
> are you now being made complete by the flesh?
> **Galatians 3:3**

This is a good point to transfer some notes into your Bible

Part 4

Jacob: Growing the Family of Faith

Crafty Brother or Leader without Guile	71
Jacob's Ladder	72
Nathanael's Mediations	73
Judah, the Line of the Messiah	76
Joseph – the World Saviour!	79
Jacob's Blessings	83
The Name of Jesus	85
The Last Word	86

Crafty Brother or Leader Without Guile

Jacob models both salvation and transformation by faith. It is not that Jacob never tries to live in blessing by his own strength, it is simply that he's not as strong as Esau and ends up having to live a different way, by faith and grace. Jacob starts by manipulating Esau's carnality and his father's frailty to steal both Esau's birthright and his blessing.

We noted above that Jacob's name comes from a root that means the lowest or last part of something, hence 'heel'. But we also know that from this image, the word could also mean 'a successor' as in someone who is at your heel, and it could mean 'crafty' as in someone who catches your heel to trip you up. In fact, the name Jacob is used to mean precisely this by Jeremiah:

> . . . do not trust any brother, because every brother deals craftily [Jacob]. **Jeremiah 9:4**

Jeremiah was speaking about those that saw Jacob's guile as a good thing, something rewarded by God and so something to be emulated. In fact Jacob was changed, both in nature and in name, to Israel, God's ruler who would always walk with a limp which presumably stopped him tripping anyone up ever again, **Genesis 32:31**.

Jacob's transformation starts with a vision at Beth-el and finishes with a Christophany at Peniel. The whole process provides the background and climax to a conversation we read in the Gospel of John, so in my Bible I've also marked the incidents are part of Jesus' teaching.

Jacob's Ladder

The story of Jacob's vision is well known. Having tricked his own Father into giving him the blessing that was meant for his brother, Esau plans to kill him, so Jacob flees eastward. En route, Jacob has his famous dream of a stairway or ladder joining heaven to earth with angels ascending and descending on it. In the morning, Jacob stands upright the stone that had been his pillow, he anoints it and calls it *Beth-El*, 'the House of God'.

 In time this anointed stone became a prophetic symbol of Solomon's temple. Some have even speculated that Jacob had his vision at Mount Moriah, the temple mount, but we don't know the location of this *Beth-el* (which we shouldn't confuse with other towns of the same name). Certainly, when Solomon's temple was built, the glory of God did descend on it, **1 Kings 8:10–11**; and, as we shall see in Volume 7, *Jesus in the United Nation*, the Temple was built to model the sleeping Jacob with his head on a stone. So prophetically, Jacob's pillow was the anointed corner stone of the House of God, prefiguring the earthly Temple, but also Jesus, **Acts 4:11**, **1 Peter 2:6–7**; and His church, **1 Peter 2:5**.

Jacob's ladder is the first 'Type of Christ' to be explicitly appropriated by Jesus. Jesus presents himself as the connection point between heaven and earth. The event is recorded in the first chapter of John's Gospel in the discussion that draws on Jacob's transformation. We will get more from Jacob's story if we take time to understand it in Jesus' story than if we just note the Type and the Theophany and move on.

Nathanael's Meditations

At the start of His ministry, Jesus is a part of the crowds that have gathered around John the Baptist. Jesus has gathered a few early followers who are interested in his ideas and in this context Philip brings a friend, Nathanael, to meet Jesus. Seeing Nathanael Jesus declares:

> See indeed an Israelite in whom there is no guile! **John 1:47**

The statement strikes Nathanael as profound and he responds with 'How do you know me?' We don't know Nathanael's private thoughts, but they must have included musings on what place cunning and guile had in being a proper son of Israel. Jeremiah had used Jacob's name to mean 'craftily' and many saw cunning as an essential Israelite quality in his day and in Jesus' too.

 Jacob, the crafty supplanter is changed after his first encounter with *YHWH* at *Beth-el,* while *YHWH* blesses him, his own uncle first cheats him and then resents him. Then on his return to face Esau and the consequences of his guileful past *YHWH* appears to him 'face to face', **Genesis 32:30**. The Bible calls this theophany *Dabar YHWH* / '*YHWH* the Word', **1 Kings 18:31**. Jacob's transformation was complete when he saw the pre-incarnate Son face to face.

Nathanael was presumably not one of those Israelites that revelled in Jacob's craftiness, so he replies to Jesus: 'How do you know me?', **John 1:48.**

Jesus continues: 'When you were under the fig tree, I saw you', which astounds Nathanael even more. He was clearly meditating as he sat under the fig tree and we can surmise some of his thinking from the way the conversation develops.

Sitting in the shade of a tree was an everyday activity, but the shade of a fig tree is used by **Micah** as an image of an age when the world would come in peace to the *Beth-el* of Jacob, the place where heaven and earth met.

Come let us go . . . to the House of the God
(*Beth-elohi* / נית-אלהי) of Jacob . . . each will *sit*
under his vine and *under his fig tree* and no one
will make them afraid . . . **Micah 4:2–4**

Now the phrase '. . . *and no one will make them afraid*'
is used again (the Hebrew is identical) in Zephaniah. This
time it describes a guileless remnant who are waiting for
YHWH who does come to them in Jerusalem.

The remnant of Israel will do no wrong and tell
no lies . . . they shall feed and lie down *and no
one will make them afraid . . . The King of Israel,
YHWH* is in your midst. **Zephaniah 3:13–15**

Nathanael sees the connections, he acknowledges Jesus
as the God-King in Zephaniah's vision: 'You are the Son of
God, you are *the King of Israel*', **John 1:49.**

Jesus concludes the dialogue by returning to guileful Jacob.
Jacob's transformation into guile-free Israel was started
at *Beth-el*, by his vision of a ladder with angels going up
and down on it, and was concluded when he saw God the
Word face to face. So Jesus promises Nathanael:

You *shall* see the heavens opened and the
angels of God ascending and descending on
the Son of Man. **John 1:51**

All of Jesus' speech and actions are steeped in Old Testament ideas and imagery; without it the New Testament record will feel thinner and less full than it should!

There are lots of details in Jacob's wider story that add depth and colour to incidents in the Gospels, for instance: Jesus meets a woman in Samaria in the land Jacob gave to Joseph as an extra portion. We read about this land in **Genesis 33:19–20** and **48:21–22**. When Jacob first purchased this land he built an altar there are gave it a name that contained 'God' in it three times: *El-El*ohe-Isra-*El* or 'God-the-God-of-God's-ruler', inadvertently reflecting the trinity, **Genesis 33:20**. Then, Rachel's death near Bethlehem giving birth to Benjamin, **Genesis 35:17–18** marks the town as a place of both joy and sorrow. But I will let you find them and mark them for yourself. In the space we have left I want to focus on the testimony in just two of Jacob's sons and then we will return to Jacob for his final blessings, death and funeral in Genesis **49** and **50**.

Judah, the Line of the Messiah

Jesus' genealogy descends through Judah, so I've highlighted **Genesis 38** which is about Judah, his children and family – a somewhat messy series of events! Judah's first son, Er, dies. His second son, Onan, is supposed to raise up an heir for his brother, as was the custom, by marrying his brother's widow, Tamar. But Onan doesn't want to and, to the embarrassment of Sunday School teachers everywhere, 'spills his seed' on the ground. Onan dies too. To cut a long story short Tamar ends up seducing her drunk Father-in-law who intends to kill her when he discovers she's pregnant, until he realises he's the father, at which point he marries her.

This is not a passage that gets preached from that often, despite the fact that Tamar is one of just five women named in Jesus' genealogy. In terms of understanding this passage, it's useful to note that there is a threat to the line that is going to produce the Messiah. Without that perspective it's hard to understand the 'sin of Onan' without drawing unhelpfully prurient conclusions.

Judah and Tamar's first son is called Perez, and before Genesis is over he has given Judah a grandson, Hezron. I mentioned at the start of this book that Judah, Perez and Hezron added to the prophecy being written by the names of Jesus' ancestors. This is a good place to return to that prophecy.

Judah: 'Judah' is usually translated as 'praise' or 'praise him'. It comes from the verb *yada* / ידה which means to acknowledge in a broad sense. The King James Bible translates it as: 'confess', **2 Chronicles 6:24**; to 'thank', **2 Samuel 22:50**; and even to 'shoot' an arrow at, **Jeremiah 50:14**; as well as to 'praise'!

Some translators also see the noun *hud* / הוד in the name. *Hud* is a uniquely Hebrew word, it is used for divine qualities such as splendour, majesty, authority etc. *YHWH* is clothed with it in **Psalm 104:1**. I like to translate 'Judah' as 'To confess his quality' though the more traditional 'confess him' or 'praise him' work fine too.

Later in life, Judah had twin sons by Tamar: Perez and Zerah.

Perez: Perez becomes the ancestor of David and ultimately Jesus. Now '*Perez*' very simply means, 'breaks-through' or 'breaks out of' or 'breeches'. Perez in turn also has two sons, Hezron and Hamul. It's Hezron who is in Jesus' line.

Hezron: '*Hezron*' means a 'walled place' or an 'enclosure'. As well as being a person, Hezron was also a walled town, which **Joshua 15:25** tells us was sometimes called Hazor which means 'Castle', making Hezron a stronghold!

So the last three patriarchs from Jesus' family tree to be found in Genesis tell us that:

> *To confess him/his quality (Judah) breaks out of (Perez) the stronghold (Hezron).*

Or as Paul puts it:

> If you confess with your mouth that Jesus [*Him*] is

Lord and believe in your heart that God raised Him
from the dead [*His quality:* i.e raised by the Father
as God's ruler], you will be saved. **Romans 10:9**

Sin and death are a prison, a stronghold we need to be
freed from, **Romans 8:2**.

There is an incident in the life of Samson where the gates
of Gaza are shut to trap him inside the Philistine city.
Samson pulls up the gate posts and drags the whole lot
up a nearby hill. Illustrating what Jesus would mean when
he stated: 'the gates of hades will not prevail against you',
Matthew 16:18.

**By the end of Genesis, Jesus' family tree has prophesied
that salvation comes by confession of Jesus and his divine
qualities!**

Joseph – The World Saviour!

Joseph's story is the longest and most detailed of any
character in Genesis. He is not a full patriarch to the whole
nation, but he does become the pre-eminent tribal head
in Israel's early history. And even though Joseph plays no
part in the Messianic family, he does reveal Jesus with
more typological points of contact than perhaps any other
character in the whole Bible. In addition, the name 'Jesus'
or ישוע is hidden twice at the end of Joseph's story.

But first, typologically Joseph's story foreshadows not just the death and resurrection of Jesus, but his ascension and return as well.

We can see Jesus' life, past, present and future in the broad brush-strokes of the story:

Death: Joseph is a late-born, favoured son, who is rejected and plotted against by his own family (the embryonic nation of Israel), who co-operate with the Gentiles in the shape of the Ishmaelite / Midianite traders and the Egyptians. Joseph is sold and left for dead.

Resurrection: Joseph experiences a resurrection and ascension to the right-hand-of-power in Egypt. But as with Jesus, while this benefits the 'gentiles' it is not recognised by his 'countrymen'. Joseph gives bread to the whole world and *saves* it from starvation.

Ascension: While in his ascended position, his own brothers start interacting with him but don't recognise him, but Joseph secretly looks after them with material wealth.

Return: Finally, Joseph's truth is revealed to his brothers, they receive his forgiveness and grace, and he is acknowledged and worshipped by them.

That's the big picture, the table on the next two pages lists the details.

Genesis Reference	Typological Parallel	New Testament Reference
Genesis 37:2	Joseph was a shepherd of his father's sheep, as was Jesus	John 10:11, 27
Genesis 37:3	Joseph was loved by his father as Jesus was loved by The Father	Matthew 3:17
Genesis 37:4	Both were rejected by their brothers	John 7:5
Genesis 37:13, 14	Joseph was sent by his father with a message for his brothers. Jesus was sent by the Father to his own	Hebrews 2:11
Genesis 37:20	Both were plotted against . . .	John 11:53
Genesis 37:23	. . . and had their robes taken from them	John 19:23
Genesis 37:25	Both were taken to Egypt	Matthew 2:14,15
Genesis 37:28	Both were sold for the price of a slave	Matthew 26:15
Genesis 39:7	Both were tempted	Matthew 4:1
Genesis 39:16–18	Both were falsely accused . . .	Matthew 26:59, 60

Genesis Reference	Typological Parallel	New Testament Reference
Genesis 39:20	. . . and bound in chains	Matthew 27:2
Genesis 40:2,3	Both were 'punished' with two others, one of whom was 'saved' and the other 'lost'	Luke 23:32
Genesis 41:41	Both were raised up after their suffering	Philippians 2:9–11
Genesis 41:46	Both were in their 30s when they started their main ministry	Luke 3:23
Genesis 45:1–15	Both forgave those that wronged them	Luke 23:34
Genesis 45:7	Both were saviours of their people (and of the whole world)	Matthew 1:21
Genesis 50:20	What Joseph recognised in his own story was ultimately more true in Jesus' – what men had worked for evil, God turned for good	1 Corinthians 2:7,8

Joseph's death is recorded in the very last verse of Genesis, **50:26**. Jacob's last word and death have been recorded in chapter **49**.

This is a good point to transfer some notes into your Bible

Jacob's blessings

As his life draws to a close, Jacob draws together his 12 sons and prophesies to each of them. The prophecies are predictive and each is worked out in the history of Israel, but those prophecies are not the point of this book series, with the exception of the word for for Judah, through whom the Messiah would come. To Judah Jacob says:

> Your father's sons shall bow down to you, Judah
> is a young lion . . . **Genesis 49:8c-9a**

. . . implying that as Judah matures, the tribe will assume the leadership of the other tribes. In time, the people of Israel become the nation of Judah and 'The Lion of Judah' becomes a messianic sigil. It is still found on the emblem of Jerusalem today, though in the book of Revelation it is Jesus who is called 'The Lion of Judah':

> And one of the elders said to me: Don't weep,
> see the Lion of the tribe of Judah, the Root of

David, has prevailed to open the book, and to break the seven seals. **Revelation 5:5**

But more specifically Jacob prophesies that:

The sceptre will not depart from Judah, nor the ruler's staff from between his feet until Shiloh comes! To him shall be the obedience of the peoples. **Genesis 49:10**

As a name, *Shiloh* has been derived from two roots. The BDB Theological Dictionary derives its meaning from *ashr / אשר* and *lu / לו*, which makes the name mean 'He whose it is', or 'He who it belongs to'. But Jones' Dictionary of Bible names derives the name from *shala / שלה* meaning 'peace'. Either way the name became a prophetic title for the Messiah and both meanings are picked up by later prophets – Ezekiel looks forward to the one '*who the right belongs to*' that will unite the priestly and kingly offices, **Ezekiel 21:27**; and Isaiah looks forward to the child who will be called '*Prince of Peace*', **Isaiah 9:6**.

Jacob's prophecy came to be understood as meaning that the rights of self-government would be continuous within Judah until the Messiah came to claim them permanently. Despite being conquered by four successive Empires, losing and regaining large amounts of territory, Judah never had a generation that wasn't led by a Jewish King, Governor or Prince. That was until 6 AD.

Herod the Great was an Edomite by descent, but his family had converted before his birth and Herod was legally Jewish. That didn't stop people speculating of course. Many considered Herod to be a non-Jew, but Jesus was born under the regency of a Jewish king albeit a bad one. When Herod the Great died Judea passed to his son Archelaus. Archelaus was as cruel as his father, he was deposed by the Romans and banished to Gaul in 6 AD. Judea was now under direct Roman rule (Galilee was still ruled by Archelaus' brother, Herod Antipas), but apart from 3 years under Herod Agrippa (41–44 AD), Judah didn't regain the 'ruler's staff' until the birth of the modern state of Israel in 1948.

Jesus was a teenager when Herod Agrippa, the last King of Judea, was born. Jacob's prophecy was fulfilled perfectly.

The name of Jesus

Genesis concludes by naming Jesus, not once but twice.

At the beginning of this book we highlighted how Jacob expresses faith in Jesus in the middle of prophesying over his sons. He prophesies to the first six and before he prophesies to the last six he states:

> I have waited for your Jesus / ישוע, *YHWH*!
> **Genesis 49:18**

Jesus / ישוע is translated here as 'salvation', which is no doubt what Jacob intended, but by faith we can see the Holy Spirit's mark in the text. It is also interesting to note that grammatically, 'salvation' is concluded with a final Tav–ת, which in ancient Hebrew was written as a cross–✕, and the word קויתי translated 'I have waited' means more literally 'I have bonded to'. So we could read Jacob's witness as:

I have bonded to your Jesus-cross, *YHWH*!

Salvation has always been by faith in the saving life of Christ. Jacob's blessing concludes with the words: 'These are the 12 tribes of Israel', **Genesis 49:28a**, the number 12 plays a cryptic role in the next chapter.

The Last Word

In **Genesis 50**, the twelve brothers are reconciled as one family as they bury Jacob. In the concluding verses of the book we find the name of Jesus again, this time coded in every twelfth letter (in reverse order) of the Hebrew text spanning verses **22** and **23**:

> Joseph lived one hundred and ten years. Joseph saw the descendants of Ephraim to the third generation. He also saw the children of Makir the son of Manasseh.

The table below shows the letters of Jesus / ישוע as they appear in the words of **Genesis 50:22–23**.

. . . and ten . . .	ועשר	ע
. . . Joseph . . .	יוסף	ו
. . . third . . .	שלשים	ש
. . . Makir . . .	מביר	י

In the first verse of Genesis we saw the hidden title for Jesus, the Aleph–א Tav–ת that became the Alpha–α Omega–ω of the last chapter of Revelation. In the penultimate chapter, we read the name Jesus in plain text. And in the final chapter, it is hidden in the tribes and generations of Israel. In the intervening stories we have seen prophecies and models of the redeemer to come. As the Bible unfolds it will put colour and details into the outline of that life and personality that mankind has owned since 'the days the Fathers fell asleep'.

This is the last point to transfer some notes into your Bible

. . . this brings us to the end of our look at the book of Genesis. We will pick up the story of Jesus in the Old Testament in the next volume:

4

Jesus in the Great Escape

Out of Egypt

Exodus

While we have come to the end of this book, I hope this is just the beginning, and acts as a springboard for you to get deeper into Scripture and find Jesus in even more wonderful ways.

Summary

In the lives of the Patriarchs we have seen Jesus revealed in many ways:

 We are given more details about the 'seed' who will inherit the earth.

 Joseph models the ascended Christ, Melchizedek models an eternal priesthood.

 Jesus' conversation with Nathanael makes sense in the light of Jacob's transformation.

 The names of Jesus' ancestors prophesy the means of salvation.

 YHWH appears as three men to Abraham.

 'The Word of *YHWH*' appears and acts for the first time.

 Truth is hidden in place names, and Jesus' name is hidden in the middle and the end of Genesis.

The Jesus Centred Bible project is constantly evolving, so if you have new ideas about how Jesus is revealed in the Bible then please get in contact through *jesuscentred.org* and join in the discussion.

Jesus in the Old Testament Series (proposed plan)

Jesus in the Old Testament: OUT
An introduction 2017
Genesis – Malachi
978-0-9933445-1-0

Jesus in the Beginning:
Creation & Primeval History
Genesis 1 – 12   OUT
978-0-9933445-5-8   2017

Jesus in the Fathers:
Patriarchs & Promises
Genesis 12 – 50   OUT
978-0-9933445-7-2   NOW

Jesus in the Great Escape:
Out of Egypt
Exodus
978-0-9933445-5-8

Jesus in the Wilderness:
Signs and Wanders
Leviticus – Deuteronomy
978-0-9933445-8-9

Jesus in War and Peace:
The Age of Heroes and Heroines
Joshua – Ruth

Jesus in the United Nation:
Under an anointed Prophet, Priest and King
1 &2 Samuel – 1 Kings

Jesus in Division and Defeat:
Prophetic Purpose in a Broken People
2 Kings – 1 & 2 Chronicles

Jesus in Words of Wisdom:
For Life, Love and Loss
Job – Song of Songs

Jesus in Worship and Wonder: OUT 2017
Melody, Mystery and the Messiah   Psalms
978-0-9933445-9-6

Jesus in the Major Prophets:
Incarnation, Crucifixion, Resurrection and Ascension
Isaiah – Daniel

Jesus in the Minor Prophets:
Revealing the Plans of God
Hosea – Malachi

Jesus in Exile and Return:
Creating a Space for Grace
Ezra – Esther + input from the prophets

Jesus in the Silent Years:
Providence inthe Wait for The Messiah
End of the Old Testament to start of the Gospels